DO WHAT
YOU LIKE

# JOBS IF YOU LIKE
# Science

Don Nardo

ReferencePoint
Press

San Diego, CA

**For more information, contact:**
ReferencePoint Press, Inc.
PO Box 27779
San Diego, CA 92198
www.ReferencePointPress.com

LIBRARY OF CONGRESS CATALOGING-IN-PUBLICATION DATA

Names: Nardo, Don, 1947- author.
Title: Jobs if you like science / Don Nardo.
Description: San Diego : ReferencePoint Press Inc., 2024. | Series: Do what you like | Includes bibliographical references and index.
Identifiers: LCCN 2024028019 (print) | LCCN 2024028020 (ebook) | ISBN 9781678209865 (library binding) | ISBN 9781678209872 (ebook)
Subjects: LCSH: Science--Vocational guidance--Juvenile literature.
Classification: LCC Q147 .N285 2024 (print) | LCC Q147 (ebook) | DDC 502.3--dc23/eng/20240624
LC record available at https://lccn.loc.gov/2024028019
LC ebook record available at https://lccn.loc.gov/2024028020

# Contents

# Introduction: Skills Needed to Tackle Unanswered Questions

"I have always been interested in the way that the Universe works," the late University of California, San Diego, astronomer Gene Smith once wrote. "There is no feeling quite like discovery, knowing some piece of the great puzzle of how the Universe works that no one else knows."[1] Michelle Thaller, an astronomer at the National Aeronautics and Space Administration's Goddard Space Center, echoes that thought, saying, "I always wanted to be an astronomer ever since I was a very small child. . . . I could just never get the questions out of my head."[2] Smith and Thaller have been far from alone in this personal yearning to tackle the unanswered questions about the world and existence. Indeed, if there is one consistent theme among scientists in general, it is the desire to investigate, and perhaps answer, some of those many unanswered questions.

There are many different approaches to that noble goal, because today there are more scientific disciplines than ever before in history. Besides astronomers, only a few of the more familiar kinds of scientists include meteorologists and other atmospheric scientists; chemists, biochemists, and physicists; geographers; paleontologists; botanists; zoologists, animal scientists, and dozens of other types of animal experts; nuclear scientists; various medical scientists; and forensic scientists (who help the police solve crimes).

A great many of the young people who desire to enter these professions do so because they, like Smith and Thaller, are fascinated by the work and the desire to expand human knowledge. But there are other reasons people choose these occupations. For instance, professional scientists tend to be well paid, as well as command respect and a certain amount of societal esteem.

Also, the job market for most types of scientists each year tends to be either stable or expanding. As the Bureau of Labor Statistics put it in 2024, "If you're interested in a science career, there's good news: many jobs in science are growing."[3] As of 2024, the scientific discipline that was growing the fastest was that of epidemiology (which investigates the incidence, spread, and control of various diseases). The need for members of that profession was growing at the rate of about 27 percent, an impressive number considering that a growth rate of 4 to 5 percent is deemed average for most occupations. A few of the other better-than-average growth rates for jobs in science include those for medical scientists (10 percent), food scientists (8 percent), animal scientists (8 percent), and biochemists (7 percent).

## Soft Skills as Important as Hard Ones

Still another reason that many young people decide to go into the sciences is that these individuals possess certain innate abilities or talents that serve those occupations well. And some of those talents can be developed into strong, useful skills as people learn more about their chosen scientific branch and begin to pursue it professionally. Such general abilities are most often classified as technical, or hard, skills. The most common one is a proficiency at, or an aptitude for, technical tasks—that is, hands-on tasks that must be learned in order to do a specific job. For a scientist, these typically include, among others, comprehending and analyzing large amounts of raw data, writing computer programs, learning to operate mechanical devices in general, and performing mathematical calculations.

However, as both the people who hire scientists and the scientists themselves point out, in today's job market, technical skills are frequently not enough. Indeed, they may not guarantee that someone with a strong interest in science will readily find a well-paying job in the sciences. According to Jared Auclair, director of the biotechnology master's program at Boston's Northeastern University, today candidates for science jobs usually need more than hard skills. They must also develop certain soft skills, he explains. Transferable to nonscientific jobs as well, soft skills are the diverse personal traits and talents related to *how* people approach their jobs. Research shows, Auclair points out, that a whopping 92 percent of hiring managers in the United States now view soft skills to be equally important as, or even more crucial than, hard skills for people looking for work in the sciences.

Among those soft skills required to become a scientist today, close to the top of the list is the ability to communicate effectively. Scientists have to be able to explain and justify their projects to those who will fund their research. Says Auclair, "You need to talk about experiments and . . . make sure you're communicating the goal, approach, and deliverables in a way that it makes sense to everyone,"[4] especially to financial backers who know little about the nitty-gritty of the science involved. Other soft skills for the sciences include adaptability, self-motivation, critical thinking, and the ability to find solutions to problems that inevitably emerge in scientific research. All and all, employment experts say, acquiring a generous mix of hard and soft skills will help teach a young, prospective scientist to think clearly and logically and make him or her an excellent candidate when job hunting in the sciences.

## What Does an Epidemiologist Do?

Epidemiologists are medical experts who, through extensive research and study, seek out and identify the causes of illnesses in a population. They also attempt to find ways to reduce the occurrence of those ills and educate the public about how to avoid them. Informally called "disease detectives," epidemiologists enjoy a great deal of latitude and flexibility in their approaches to fighting disease outbreaks and in the kinds of settings they work in. "The thing about epidemiology," remarks Dale Sandler, chief epidemiologist at the National Institute of Environmental Health Sciences in Durham, North Carolina, "is it's a career that can go in many different directions. There are epidemiologists who work in hospitals and in infection control. And there are people who work at the CDC [Centers for Disease Control and Prevention] who work in the really exciting area of trying to track down outbreaks of infectious or noninfectious illnesses."[5]

One of the many exciting stories of these disease detectives tracking down horrible ailments and saving thousands (and in some cases millions) of lives involves the mystery of the spread of the dreaded Ebola virus. In 2014 almost thirty thousand people in

### A Few Facts

**Typical Earnings**
$85,000 on average

**Educational Requirements**
Master's degree or higher

**Personal Qualities**
Ability to spot patterns in large amounts of data

**Work Settings**
Offices, laboratories, and sometimes in the field

**Future Outlook**
Growth rate of 27 percent through 2032

West Africa contracted this disease. Highly contagious, its symptoms include fever, vomiting, diarrhea, and liver failure. Local doctors could not figure out how the illness was quickly spreading across thousands of square miles, so epidemiologists from several countries went to Africa to help.

Among those intrepid disease detectives was an Australian, Katrina Roper. Initially, she and her colleagues were stumped. How, they wondered, could farmers working their lands in one area spread the contagion to farmers who lived hundreds of miles away? In an effort to answer that question, the epidemiologists interviewed hundreds of people—asking them to describe their movements over a period of weeks, detailing where they traveled, and when. The epidemiologists then used this information to create detailed maps of people's movements. The investigators also examined samples of the Ebola virus in areas hundreds of miles apart to see how it mutated, or changed, as it spread. In these ways, Roper and her colleagues traced the locals' daily and weekly activities and discovered the highly complex ways that the virus spread from one person to another, from village to village, and from country to country.

In similar ways, over time, epidemiologists have identified how numerous other dread diseases spread. These include cholera, hepatitis A, sleeping sickness, and HIV (which causes AIDS). The work is often exhilarating, says former epidemiologist Seema Yasmin. "There's the thrill of chasing mysterious microbes, identifying patient zero in an outbreak, and the lifelong friendships that are formed along the way."[6]

## A Typical Workday

Workdays for epidemiologists can vary considerably. When trying to discover how a disease spreads, for instance, epidemiologists mght spend hours developing strategies for tracking the illness. They might then travel to the region where the outbreak has occurred. Once there, they will collect evidence—possibly including soil samples, animal droppings, plant specimens, and human blood. Next, these disease detectives will interview local residents to trace their daily and weekly movements. They will eventually return to the laboratory to study the collected evidence and determine how the disease has been spreading. Finally, the epidemiologists will brief local officials on the findings and help educate the locals on how to avoid contracting the disease.

## Education and Training

A person who wants to become an epidemiologist must first get a bachelor's degree, and then a master's degree or higher. According to the Bureau of Labor Statistics (BLS), most epidemiologists obtain bachelor's degrees in biology, public policy and social services, or social science. Individual courses within those fields typically include ones in public health, medical and other physical science topics, various aspects of mathematics, and studies in statistics.

The most common field chosen for a master's degree is public health, which at many colleges can include specific courses

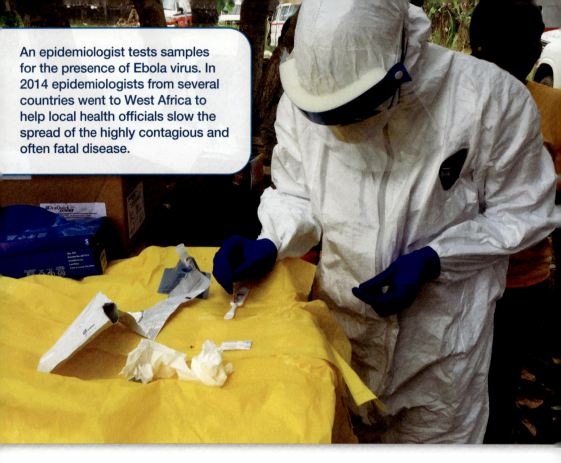

An epidemiologist tests samples for the presence of Ebola virus. In 2014 epidemiologists from several countries went to West Africa to help local health officials slow the spread of the highly contagious and often fatal disease.

in epidemiology and related medical topics. In addition, the BLS points out, "Master's degree programs in public health, as well as other programs that are specific to epidemiology, may require students to complete an internship . . . that typically ranges in length from a semester to a year."[7]

Some of those who get a master's degree in epidemiology go on to obtain a doctorate, or PhD, in that science. However, generally a doctorate is not required to get hired as an entry-level epidemiologist.

## Skills and Personality

In their ongoing quest to understand how diseases spread and their efforts to keep the public safe from those ailments, epidemiologists frequently deal with matters of life and death. And with human life in the balance, there is very little room for inefficiency and error. Thus, these disease detectives require a number of hard and soft skills that will ensure that their work is of the highest possible quality.

Among the most common of the hard skills in question is excellent reading comprehension. Epidemiologists routinely read huge amounts of scientific literature, including long reports summarizing medical and environmental studies, articles in medical and other scientific journals, and so forth. It is crucial that large amounts of technically oriented data be absorbed and remembered. This is because recalling a few key details from a report read in the past might allow an epidemiologist to identify or halt the spread of a severe or fatal illness.

Another hard skill that is common among epidemiologists is the ability to analyze and organize large amounts of technical data, enabling them to recognize patterns in how illnesses are contracted and spread. Related to this ability to analyze data is a strong grasp of basic math and statistical concepts. This skill, medical writer Ingrid Monteiro explains, allows epidemiologists "to identify relationships between various environmental and risk factors and disease patterns and make predictions. They regularly study large datasets to determine health policy recommendations."[8]

Among the soft skills that are important for epidemiologists to have is critical thinking—the ability to choose the right course of action when confronted by a range of options presented by collected data. Communication skills are also imperative for people in this profession because they must be able to explain their methods and findings to other scientists, public officials, and those who fund epidemiological research.

## Working Conditions

The diverse duties and specialties of epidemiologists ensure that their work environments often vary, depending on the projects they are working on at any given time. Work settings can range from offices, to laboratories, to lecture halls, to governmental meetings, to a wide variety of outdoor settings (forests, jungles, farmlands, urban areas, and so forth) in countries around the world.

## Employers and Earnings

According to the BLS, roughly ten thousand epidemiologists were employed in the United States in 2022–2023. They worked for a variety of employers and organizations. According to the BLS, about 36 percent of epidemiologists worked for state governments, roughly 21 percent worked for local governments, and another 12 percent worked in hospitals. The rest of American epidemiologists did research of various kinds for universities, health insurance providers, pharmaceutical companies, or large federal agencies. Of the latter, the three largest were the CDC, National Institutes of Health, and US Environmental Protection Agency.

The salaries that epidemiologists earn can vary considerably, depending on location, experience, and skill level. Some states pay epidemiologists more than others. In 2023–2024, the District of Columbia, New Jersey, Massachusetts, California, and Washington paid members of the profession the most. An epidemiologist who has a doctorate degree earns more than someone with a master's degree. And more experience usually translates to higher pay.

According to the popular employment marketplace ZipRecruiter, in 2023–2024 the lowest salary for an epidemiologist in the United States was about $49,000 and the highest was roughly $145,000. Most of those in the profession made $70,000 to $110,000, with the median salary being about $85,000.

## Future Outlook

The BLS and other agencies and companies that track US employment figures and trends all agree that the outlook for epidemiologists in the near future is exceptionally bright. The BLS estimates that the number of jobs in the profession will grow by 27 percent through 2032, far faster than the average growth rate for all occupations. Indeed, it is projected that there will be at least eight hundred openings for epidemiologists during each calendar year until 2032.

One reason that so many new epidemiologists will be needed is to replace those who retire from the profession or switch to a different occupation. Another reason for the growing demand is that health care knowledge and technology are advancing rapidly. And one result is the ongoing discovery of new and emerging diseases. In turn, more epidemiologists will be required to study those ailments and develop ways to keep members of the public from contracting them. Overall, the extremely positive outlook for epidemiology in the mid-2020s and beyond is one reason that the 2023 jobs report for *U.S. News & World Report* chose that profession as the number one science-related job.

# Find Out More

## Centers for Disease Control and Prevention (CDC)

www.cdc.gov

The CDC's extensive website provides detailed information about outbreaks of infectious diseases around the world and what epidemiologists and other scientists are doing to keep the public safe. The website also lists travel restrictions intended to minimize such outbreaks, as recommended by epidemiologists.

## International Epidemiological Association (IEA)

https://ieaweb.org

The IEA is a global organization with branches in more than one hundred countries. Its goal is to promote communication among epidemiologists around the world. The IEA website contains a section titled "Early Career Epidemiologists" for people just starting out in this career field.

## Society for Epidemiologic Research (SER)

https://epiresearch.org

The SER promotes and supports research in epidemiology. The organization's website includes information, resources, and networking opportunities that allow students studying epidemiology to both do meaningful research and to exchange ideas with other students and with professionals.

# Computer Hardware Engineer

## What Does a Computer Hardware Engineer Do?

Computer hardware engineers, also called computer engineers, do research on, create designs for, and build prototypes of computer hardware systems or subsystems. Typical among those computer components are networks, processors, power supply units, memory devices, circuit boards (or motherboards), video cards, and routers. Such engineers also test those devices, analyze the test results, and modify the initial designs when needed. When the designs have been finalized, they are sent to a manufacturer, which builds and distributes the components. A computer hardware engineer usually oversees the manufacturing process to make sure it goes smoothly.

Some computer hardware engineers work for computer companies and are given specific tasks to do that improve the company's products. It can be stimulating, satisfying work, according to Apple hardware engineer Ashwini Simha. Her main job is to find ways to make Apple computers run as fast as possible, including eliminating whatever problems make them run too slowly. She describes her work this way: "I find issues, do a ton of investigation, get to the bottom of

### A Few Facts

**Typical Earnings**
$138,000 a year on average

**Educational Requirements**
Bachelor's degree or higher

**Personal Qualities**
Creativity and innate talent for solving problems

**Work Settings**
Mostly offices or factories

**Future Outlook**
Growth rate of 5 percent through 2032

the problem and find ways to fix it. You could say, sort of like a detective! I'm really proud of what I do every day—making Macs run fast. When I walk into a coffee shop and see almost every person with a Macbook, it's really rewarding."[9]

Computer hardware engineers do not design the software programs that run on the hardware devices. Those programs are created by computer software engineers. In some companies, hardware and software engineers work together in order to make the use of their computer systems as efficient and reliable as possible.

## A Typical Workday

Workdays for computer hardware engineers can vary, depending on the size of the company, the number of hardware engineers employed there, and the type of devices those engineers are working on at a given time. As computer and electrical engineer Dave Haynie puts it, "It depends on the day, and where things are on whatever projects there are. And of course, the specifics are different at different companies. Some have dozens or even hundreds of hardware people. At my company, I'm the primary hardware engineer and the only computer hardware engineer."[10]

In addition to designing and building prototypes of computer components, computer engineers sometimes spend days or weeks trying to solve problems encountered in the design process. Many also work with artificial intelligence (AI) and robotics. AI technology, including machine learning, is advancing rapidly. And computer companies are eager to include that new technology in their products. According to science writer James M. Tobin, at times computer engineers may on a daily basis "develop, create, test, and manage intelligent machines or robotic systems. In this role, professionals may conduct research on robotics and robot development. . . . Research is [also] ongoing in areas such as data science, machine learning . . . and human-robot interaction."[11]

## Education and Training

In most cases, entry-level computer hardware engineers require a bachelor's degree in computer engineering, computer science, electrical engineering, information technology, or a related field. A solid background in math and science provides good preparation for this coursework. Most hardware engineers also take a few computer science courses to become familiar with computer programming.

With rapid advances in computer and AI technologies, some of the bigger, better-known companies also require a master's degree. Another possible way for engineering candidates to keep up with advancing technology is to acquire part-time work experience while attending college or soon after graduating. "As you complete your degree," writes modern technology expert Aaron Kim,

> consider applying for an internship or volunteering in a hardware engineering role to gain some entry-level work experience. Gaining experience early can help you apply

concepts from your education, develop skills, and receive valuable training, which can increase your overall employability. Internships also help you find a mentor, increase your professional network and better familiarize yourself with the field.[12]

## Skills and Personality

Computer hardware engineering requires a healthy mix of hard and soft skills. One of the most important basic hard skills is a general familiarity with computers and how they operate, including the ability to recognize and correct common problems. Beyond that, computer hardware engineers must be totally conversant in the standard programming languages, such as Java, SQL, Python, and HTML. A strong grasp of primary engineering design principles is also important. Another hard skill is knowledge of the principal computer operating systems, including Windows, Linux, and Unix. An understanding of computer circuit design is still another necessary hard skill that beginners in the profession must acquire.

Also important for computer hardware engineers are several soft skills, one of the chief examples being the ability to understand and analyze complex electronic equipment. Other soft skills computer engineers should have are a talent for solving problems; creativity, which helps in fashioning new designs; a tendency to think clearly and recognize and correct one's own mistakes; and a capacity to communicate and work well with others. Regarding the latter skill, Kim states, "Computer hardware engineers may collaborate with a variety of clients and colleagues, including software developers, project managers, and research scientists. It's beneficial when they have strong teamwork skills and the ability to work effectively with others to achieve shared goals."[13]

Computer hardware engineers research, design, build, and test computer systems. In doing this they work with computer components such as processors, power supply units, memory devices, circuit boards, video cards, and routers.

## Working Conditions

With rare exceptions, computer hardware engineers work indoors. And most often they do so in office settings, although an increasing number of them work remotely at least part of the time. For the most part, they put in a traditional forty-hour workweek. But it is not unusual for computer engineers to put in extra hours when in the midst of a big project.

## Employers and Earnings

According to the Bureau of Labor Statistics (BLS), about 78,100 computer hardware engineers held jobs in the United States in 2022–2023. Roughly 20 percent of them worked for companies that do research and development in engineering and the life sciences. Another 16 percent were hired by companies that manufacture computer and other electronic components. And roughly 15 percent were designers and prototype builders for corporations that make computers and computer networks. Most of the rest oversaw or updated computer systems for the federal government and state and local governments.

The BLS reckons that in 2023 the median yearly salary of a computer hardware engineer was about $138,000. Also in 2023, the lowest-paid 10 percent of computer hardware engineers earned a bit less than $82,000 annually, whereas the highest-paid 10 percent made somewhat more than $213,000 per year. Furthermore, most of the highest-paid computer engineers worked in research and development, while the lowest-paid members of the profession worked for the federal government.

## Future Outlook

According to several agencies and companies that track employment numbers, including the BLS and the job search website Indeed, projected job openings for computer hardware engineers will likely increase by about 5 percent per year through 2032. That is within the range of the national average growth rate of 5 to 8 percent per year for all occupations. During the 2024–2032 period, experts say, on average about forty-six hundred new computer hardware engineers will be needed each year.

The BLS points out that some of those openings will occur when existing engineers retire or leave the labor force for other reasons. Other jobs for computer engineers will open up because the demand for newly designed, more advanced computer and electronic components will rise in the years ahead. Many of those components will be needed for the increasingly complex circuitry of cars, medical devices, and household appliances.

Whatever positive employment opportunities and salaries the occupation of computer hardware engineer will feature in the coming years, experienced, highly motivated engineers will have a potent added benefit. According to the BLS, hardworking members of the profession can choose to pursue new careers in closely related fields that involve computer hardware. One of those fields, the BLS says, is that of information research scientists; they "design innovative uses for new and existing computing technology." Similarly, "computer and information systems managers plan, coordinate, and direct computer-related activities in an organization, [and] computer network architects design and implement data communication networks."[14] Thus, in at least the near future, eager, well-trained computer engineers will have ample opportunities to find well-paying work.

## Find Out More

### Association for Computing Machinery (ACM)
www.acm.org
The ACM is the world's biggest scientific computing association, and part of its mission is to advance the science of computing. Its extensive website contains articles about advances in computing and information about educational opportunities for people interested in computer technology.

**Institute of Electrical and Electronics Engineers (IEEE)**

www.ieee.org

The IEEE says that its main mission is to spur technological innovation, including that related to computers and other modern electrical devices, for the overall benefit of humanity. Its website offers information on educational programs for various kinds of engineers and alerts members to upcoming conferences worldwide.

**Society of Women Engineers (SWE)**

https://swe.org

Already in its seventh decade, the SWE promotes the education and hiring of women engineers, including computer engineers. The website features information about educational opportunities, including scholarships, for female engineers.

# Microbiologist

## What Does a Microbiologist Do?

Microbiologists study microscopic life forms (also called microbes or germs). These include bacteria, viruses, algae, and fungi, among others. The structure, reproduction, growth, and other characteristics of those tiny creatures, as well as how they sometimes cause disease, all fall under the purview of microbiologists. Within their scientific discipline, they sometimes employ narrower specialties that concentrate on one kind of microbe or a specific aspect of microbes in general. For example, microbiologists who concentrate only on bacteria are known as bacteriologists. Similarly, mycologists are microbiologists who specialize in fungi, such as molds and yeasts. And medical microbiologists concentrate mainly on how germs cause various diseases.

Microbes are essential to all life, but they can also be harmful. University of South Alabama microbiologist Mary Burtnick studies disease-causing bacteria, or more simply, how bacteria make people sick. She explains her latest project:

We are currently working on a very interesting project focusing on a recently described bacterial secretion system. Bacteria are thought to utilize this

## A Few Facts

**Typical Earnings**
$85,000 on average

**Educational Requirements**
Bachelor's degree or higher

**Personal Qualities**
Detail oriented, curious, observant, creative

**Work Settings**
Offices, laboratories, and outdoors

**Future Outlook**
Growth rate of 5 percent through 2032

secretion system to inject specific molecules into host cells. We don't know yet exactly how this system functions, but we have many experiments planned to try to figure it out. This is of particular interest to me because it is a relatively new area of study and there are many unanswered questions.[15]

## A Typical Workday

Because the studies and duties of microbiologists are so numerous and often extremely varied, it is difficult to categorize any given day as typical. Only two of the duties involved include planning and performing diverse laboratory experiments and going out in the field to collect specimens of microbes found in the soil, in lakes, on plants and animals, and on and inside people. Other common duties are to identify such specimens using powerful microscopes and to organize and maintain the microbes in cultures. Microbiologists also regularly write reports about their work and give lectures summarizing their findings. Burtnick adds that she spends a lot of her time "designing and carrying out experiments, keeping up to date with the current microbiology literature, meeting with colleagues, writing . . . grant applications, as well as [teaching] microbiology classes."[16]

## Education and Training

In most cases, a prospective microbiologist requires a bachelor's degree. It can be in microbiology specifically, or it can be in a related field, such as biology, microbial science, or biomedical science. However, although some organizations or labs will accept a bachelor's degree, others may prefer the candidate have a master's degree or even a PhD.

Whatever degree level would-be microbiologists may be pursuing, among the courses they will be required to take are chem-

Microbiologists study microscopic life forms, such as bacteria and viruses that cause disease. Sometimes they collect the specimens that they will then analyze in a laboratory.

istry, physics, various math courses, environmental microbiology, genetics, bacteriology, and virology (the study of viruses). Also required is a certain amount of laboratory experience, including work with advanced microscopes and creating microbial cultures in the lab. In some cases university students who excel at lab work might be offered brief internships, in which they assist established scientists. Those who hire microbiologists tend to look favorably at individuals with such internships under their belts.

## Skills and Personality

Not surprisingly, considering how technically oriented microbiology is and the enormous amount of precise, detailed scientific information it encompasses, prospective microbiologists need to possess or develop certain hard skills. These include the ability to use a wide range of laboratory equipment, strong mathematical skills, and knowledge of diverse natural environments and the ability to monitor them to determine the roles that microbes play in them. Another technical skill needed is a working knowledge of good manufacturing practices to comply with government and industry standards for handing potentially dangerous microbes.

Many soft skills are also needed to achieve success as a microbiologist. For instance, a person must be detail oriented, because both observation of and experimentation with microscopic organisms requires extreme precision. The Bureau of Labor Statistics (BLS) also stresses the importance of logical-thinking skills, saying that "microbiologists draw conclusions from experiments by using reasoning and judgment to interpret the results." A healthy portion of perseverance is also beneficial, the BLS states, because microbiologists "must persist in the trial-and-error demands of research [and] they should be motivated to avoid becoming discouraged in their work."[17]

Another soft skill a successful microbiologist should possess is adeptness at communicating with colleagues, bosses, and sometimes the media (if and when important discoveries are made). Interacting with colleagues can be especially important, as well as stimulating, Burtnick points out. She says that she enjoys "the collaborative nature of research. By working together with other scientists, we can use our combined expertise to solve problems. Sometimes when experiments aren't working, advice from a colleague or coworker can help you look at the problem from a completely different angle."[18]

Other soft skills a microbiologist will benefit from are certain positive personality traits. One is a talent for solving problems, because difficulties and complications are par for the course in laboratory work. Burtnick describes a few other such valuable personal traits:

> In order to succeed as a scientific researcher, you need to be focused, dedicated, inquisitive, and enthusiastic about what you are studying. You also need to be creative and learn to think outside the box. I enjoy . . . performing experiments, especially when an experiment results in new or unexpected data; this can be really exciting at times and can make us think about a problem or a question in different ways.[19]

## Working Conditions

The settings in which most microbiologists work can vary. Although they do tend to spend a fair amount of time doing lab work, the image of them confined mainly to the laboratory is a stereotype. A majority of microbiologists have offices, for instance, where they write reports, plan new projects, and meet with colleagues. And many members of the profession travel, sometimes widely, to collect microbial samples. Also, some microbiologists are professors in colleges and universities, while still others work in factory settings, notably facilities where food products containing microbes are prepared.

## Employers and Earnings

According to the BLS and other agencies that keep track of employment figures, in 2022–2023 there were roughly 20,900 microbiologists working in the United States. Close to a third of them conducted research for food and bottled beverage companies that need to make sure their products are free of dangerous microbes. Others in this group worked for biofuels businesses that use microbes in the manufacturing process. Another 20 percent or so of microbiologists worked for departments or agencies of the federal government, including the Centers for Disease Control and Prevention and National Institutes of Health. Roughly 15 percent, or about 3,100 of the 20,900 microbiologists, worked for pharmaceutical firms and companies that manufacture medicines. And more than 1,200 members of the profession taught in colleges, universities, and professional schools.

The BLS reports that in 2023 the median yearly wage for microbiologists was about $85,000. The lowest-paid 10 percent of them made about $49,000 or less, and the highest-paid 10 percent earned a bit more than $147,000. In that same year, the median annual salary for microbiologists who worked for the federal government was approximately $100,000, whereas the median yearly income of microbiologists who taught in colleges and universities was $63,000.

## Future Outlook

According to the BLS, the number of jobs available for microbiologists each year in the United States will likely grow by about 5 percent through 2032. Also, there should be an average of roughly seventeen hundred job openings for microbiologists each year. Some of those openings will occur when veteran microbiologists either retire or leave the labor force for other reasons.

## What Microbiology Can Tell Us

"I have always wondered why one person, exposed to a pathogen, gets terribly sick while another person does not. Scientists have been working on infectious diseases for many years and still have very few explanations for why this can occur. I strongly suspect the oral microbiome [all of the microbes in the mouth] may allow us to finally gain some insights on this tricky subject."

—Camille Zenobia, microbiologist

Quoted in Anne O. Rice, "An Interview with Microbiologist Camille Zenobia, PhD, 'Oral Health Activist,'" RDH, March 3, 2023. www.rdhmag.com.

Experts add that the profession of microbiology will likely attract at least some people in each new generation for a less practical reason—that the world of microbes is largely a mysterious realm that requires powerful microscopes to see. Also, both very good and very bad germs exist simultaneously in nature. Put simply, these realities tend to fascinate some people. One prominent example is Dave Westenberg, a microbiologist who teaches at the Missouri University of Science and Technology. He calls himself a "germ juggler" because of the strange duality that some microbes are essential to human well-being, whereas others are very dangerous. "Trying to balance that [odd truth]," he says, "becomes a juggling act."[20]

## Find Out More

**American Society for Microbiology (ASM)**

https://asm.org

Founded in 1899, the ASM is made up of microbiologists and other scientists around the world whose work touches on germs. Through holding meetings and sharing knowledge, they strive to make life safer for people everywhere by learning more about microbes. The ASM website contains helpful links to sources of information about how to become a microbiologist.

## International Union of Microbiological Societies (IUMS)
https://iums.org
The IUMS promotes research into fighting microbes that cause infectious diseases, while learning more about how other microbes benefit people and animals. Its website offers information about upcoming meetings of microbiologists worldwide, as well as highlights articles and books written by IUMS members.

## National Institute of Allergy and Infectious Diseases (NIAID)
www.niaid.nih.gov
A subdivision of the National Institutes of Health, the NIAID strongly supports research into microbes that leads to a fuller understanding of how to treat and prevent infectious diseases. The website features news about recent scientific discoveries and information about how to get research projects funded.

# Animal Scientist

## What Does an Animal Scientist Do?

Animal scientists study and advance knowledge of animals, mostly livestock found on ranches and farms. These animals include chickens, ducks, pigs, sheep, and cows that are raised for meat or provide other products, including milk, eggs, and wool. Also included are farm animals used in breeding. In addition, animal scientists study animals such as horses and greyhounds that are used in racing.

In general, animal scientists want to learn as much as possible about how these creatures reproduce, what is best for them to eat, what diseases they are susceptible to, and how they interact with or are essential to human society. Most animal scientists tend to specialize in their approaches to learning about domestic animals. For instance, some members of the profession opt to study these creatures by examining them, their deoxyribonucleic acid (DNA) and other aspects of their physiology, and the diseases that affect them, in laboratory settings. There, they do research and perform experiments under strictly controlled conditions.

In contrast, a good many animal scientists spend much of their

### A Few Facts

**Typical Earnings**
$72,000 on average

**Educational Requirements**
Bachelor's degree, or higher

**Personal Qualities**
Ability to analyze data; communication and critical-thinking skills

**Work Settings**
Farms, ranches, labs, college classes, government agencies

**Future Outlook**
Growth rate of 8 to 10 percent through the 2030s

time visiting ranches and farms. There they study the animals' lives firsthand, as well as work with the owners and managers to find the most efficient methods and practices for raising them. A notable example is animal scientist Lauren Wesolowski. In 2021–2022, while still in graduate school, she visited various ranches to study the immune systems of horses up close, hoping to improve their overall health. In short order she did what experts in the field called groundbreaking work. As her college supervisor put it, she displayed "her dedication to pushing the boundaries of our understanding of equine physiology and performance. Most of the research procedures in this project had never been used in horses. Therefore, not only did Lauren perform a highly relevant and impactful study, but her findings could also shape the future of equine training and feeding programs."[21]

## A Typical Workday

There is no typical workday or work schedule for animal scientists in general. This is because they do their jobs in a wide variety of settings and have extremely varied duties, research projects, and career paths. Some animal scientists, for example, are concerned with finding improved ways of breeding horses, cows, and other farm animals in order to produce bigger, healthier offspring. Other animal scientists focus on the nutritional needs of animals, especially those raised on farms and ranches. Meanwhile, some animal scientists travel from state to state to teach farmers and ranchers the latest, most efficient ways to care for their animals. Still other animal scientists choose to prepare the next generation of their profession by teaching animal science in colleges and universities. Clearly, the workdays and work schedules of these diverse kinds of animal scientists will vary considerably.

## Improving Animal Health

"We're working a lot on . . . dietary supplement[s] . . . They not only are going to help with performance, but also stress and challenges. Animals, like humans, get stressed and secrete the hormone cortisone. This causes internal inflammation and issues with our normal oxidative balance. That leads to age lines, gray hair, all of that. Do we care if our animals get gray hair? Probably not as much as ourselves, but we are working on ways to provide nutrition that improves their health and longevity."

—Troy Wistuba, vice president of Feed & Additive Technical Innovation, Purina Animal Nutrition Center

Quoted in Careers Blog, Land O'Lakes, "An Innovative Career with Purina— Meet Dr. Troy Wistuba," 2023. https://careers.landolakesinc.com.

## Education and Training

At a minimum, someone who aspires to become an animal scientist needs a bachelor's degree. However, some research labs, colleges, and companies prefer that the person have a master's degree. In many cases, while working toward their degree, prospective animal scientists obtain practical experience by working on a farm or ranch or for a company that employs animal scientists. This allows such students to develop important skills that supplement what they are learning in their college classes.

In pursuing a bachelor's or master's degree, an aspiring animal scientist will need to take a wide range of courses, many of them specifically related to animals. According to the popular online employment portal Indeed, those courses typically include biology, laboratory science, anatomy, physiology, chemistry, statistics, animal reproduction and behavior, and livestock production, among several others.

## Skills and Personality

As is the case with all occupations in the sciences, to succeed in their jobs animal scientists need both hard and soft skills. High on the list of the hard skills is the ability to understand and analyze large amounts of technical data. A familiarity with scientific laboratory equipment and procedures is also helpful, as is proficiency in using computers.

Among the several soft skills that are beneficial to someone who wants to become an animal scientist are strong reading comprehension and both written and oral communication. Typically, a person in the profession needs to read many books, articles, and reports, not only in school but also on the job, where extra learning and training continue throughout his or her career. Also, an animal scientist must be able to confer with, learn from, and educate farmers, animal breeders, and/or managers and workers at companies that make animal feeds. Other important soft skills an animal scientist should possess or develop are attention to detail, critical thinking, and an innate capacity to solve problems.

## Employers and Work Settings

The work settings of animal scientists can vary appreciably, depending on who they work for. Some of them work on farms or for professional animal breeders. And some animal scientists work in large industrial-scale facilities that house thousands of animals. Other animal scientists can be found working in labs or classrooms in universities and other research institutions, diverse government agencies, pharmaceutical companies, and various private industries.

Animal scientists who work for large pharmaceutical corporations strive to help those companies develop and test new animal medicines and vaccines. Animal scientists in those settings also oversee or help with clinical trials involving animals and medicines. When doing so, the animal scientists typically work alongside veterinarians and other scientists concerned with the efficiency and safety of such products.

## Earnings

Regarding earnings, the Bureau of Labor Statistics (BLS) estimates that animal scientists in the lowest-paid 10 percent or so make about $46,000 per year and those in the highest-paid 10 percent or so earn roughly $121,000 a year. The average falls in the range of $72,000, which is the rough equivalent of $35 per hour. Experts say that part of this wide range of earnings is attributable to educational levels. That is, animal scientists whose earnings fall into the range's lower level tend to be those with a minimal education, compared to those with a master's degree or higher, who are at the high end of salary range.

## Future Outlook

With farms, agribusinesses, universities, pharmaceutical companies, and government agencies regularly hiring animal scientists, the need for newcomers in that field remains steady. According to the BLS and some other leading sources of employment information, there were approximately thirty-two hundred animal scientists in the United States in 2023. Estimates for the growth rate for the profession through the 2030s range from 8 to 10 percent, which is well above the average growth rate of US jobs in general.

A major reason for the steady and healthy growth rate for the profession is that technology and new discoveries related to animals are advancing rapidly. This makes animal science a good choice of occupation for people who both love animals and want a job with a bright future. According to the Michigan State University's animal science department:

> The rate of technological innovations in animal agriculture has accelerated in the last 20 years. Technology is revolutionizing animal production, research, and marketing capabilities. Over the last century, advances in animal feeding, breeding, reproduction, and management techniques occurred simultaneously with improvement in other agricultural practices. . . . Animal Science is an exciting field that has applications to all animals and provides opportunities from production through agribusiness and processing. It can provide a solid foundation for diverse careers and professional schools such as human and veterinary medicine, or graduate school.[22]

## Find Out More

**American Association for Laboratory Animal Science (AALAS)**
www.aalas.org
The AALAS is an organization of medical professionals from around the world who advocate for the humane care and treatment of lab animals. The website features information about how

to become an animal or lab scientist, as well as how to get the organization's three colorful periodic publications.

## American Society of Animal Science (ASAS)

www.asas.org

The ASAS holds that animals are crucial to humanity, and to that end it works to support research into ways to use animals in humane, responsible ways. The ASAS website includes a guide to taking care of animals in ethical ways and resources for students who are considering entering the field of animal science.

## American Veterinary Medical Association (AVMA)

www.avma.org

The AVMA's mission is to advance the science of veterinary medicine to improve the health of both animals and people. Its website contains extensive information about how interested young people can go about becoming veterinarians.

# Robotics Engineer

## What Does a Robotics Engineer Do?

Robotics engineers design, construct, and program robots of various kinds. According to CareerExplorer, a leading online source of information about US jobs:

> These engineers work at the intersection of mechanical, electrical, and computer engineering to create machines capable of performing tasks autonomously or semiautonomously. Robotics engineers are involved in the entire lifecycle of robotic systems, from conceptualization and design to programming, testing, and deployment. They may work on a wide range of applications, including industrial automation, medical robotics, autonomous vehicles, and consumer electronics.[23]

The scientific field of robotics is advancing swiftly and frequently produces innovations that are to one degree or another transforming diverse industries. These industries include manufacturing, health care, transportation systems, and space exploration,

## A Few Facts

**Typical Earnings**
$88,000 on average

**Educational Requirements**
Bachelor's degree or higher

**Personal Qualities**
Analytical thinking, problem-solving ability, aptitude for mathematics and science

**Work Settings**
Offices, laboratories, factories, university classrooms

**Future Outlook**
Growth rate of 9 percent into the 2030s

among others. In the case of space, for instance, the online site Robotics Career explains that robotics now plays a critical role:

> Space exploration requires robots that can perform complex tasks in challenging environments, such as on other planets or in space. Robotics engineers design and program these robots to perform tasks such as collecting samples, analyzing data, and conducting experiments. These robots must be able to withstand extreme temperatures, radiation, and other environmental factors that could damage their systems. NASA's [the National Aeronautics and Space Administration's] Mars rover, for example, was designed and programmed by robotics engineers to explore the surface of Mars, collecting data and images that have greatly expanded our understanding of the planet.[24]

## A Typical Workday

Given that robotics engineers work in all sorts of industries and create a wide variety of robots, it is difficult to describe a typical day for members of this profession. The duties and activities of one robotics engineer will usually differ significantly from those of many of his or her colleagues. Some build robotic arms that manipulate products in food processing and packaging plants, for example. Others design and construct artificial limbs for people who have lost a leg or an arm.

Still other robotics engineers design tiny robotic systems that will be installed in spacecraft. One of them is NASA mechanical engineer and robotics designer Christine Fuller, who spends a great deal of her time most workdays doing zero-gravity testing of robots so tiny they can fit in the palm of someone's hand. Yet like so many other types of robotics engineers, her duties can be quite varied on a daily or weekly basis. "One thing I love about my job," she says, "is that there is no typical work day. Some days I'm . . . designing a folding robot or . . . laying out traces [components making up] a Printed Circuit Board (PCB). An hour later I could be laser cutting new mounts or disassembling a joint for repair. The next day I could be in a lava tube with a robot climbing up the wall.[25]

Indeed, for Fuller and other robotics engineers, workdays can vary quite a bit. These engineers might be involved in research on the strength of various metals that will be used in robot construction. Or they might have a role in designing or installing software that tells the robot how to operate. They might also help design safety measures.

## Education and Training

A person who wants to go into robotics should take as many science and math courses as possible—starting in high school. Algebra, trigonometry, physics, computer science, and even computer-aided design classes provide essential background.

High school robotics clubs or teams are a great way to learn and get practical experience. Such groups have multiplied in recent years and have created a number of robots of astounding sophistication. In April 2024, for example, the RoboLancers team from Philadelphia's Central High School won first place in the prestigious worldwide FIRST Robotics Competition, held in Houston, Texas. Beating out some thirty-five hundred American and international teams, the RoboLancers created a robot designed to play a musical game called Crescendo. The bumper-car-shaped gadget collected numerous small objects shaped like musical notes and, to cheers from thousands of onlookers, carried them onto a raised stage.

After graduating from high school, the prospective robotics engineer should obtain a bachelor's degree, which is the minimum educational level needed to be hired in the robotics field. The four-year bachelor's degree can be in electronic engineering or mechanical engineering, although some universities now have full-fledged robotics majors. Whatever major the person opts for, must-take courses will include trigonometry, calculus, and other advanced math courses; physics; computer science; computer programming; biology; chemistry; artificial intelligence; and drafting. Those who hope to advance in their careers will likely need to get a master's degree or doctorate.

## Skills and Personality

As in all the sciences, skills and abilities in robotics engineering fall into two categories—hard and soft. Among the hard skills are an aptitude for understanding scientific, mathematical, and engineering principles, as well as a strong ability to work with computers. Some of the more important soft skills that benefit robot-

Robotics engineers design, build, and program robots that are used for many different purposes. They also test robots in the field (as pictured here) to make sure they are working properly.

ics engineers are creativity, solid problem-solving skills, and good communication skills. The latter skill is especially vital because it is common for a robotics engineer to work as part of a team.

In more general terms, CareerExplorer suggests that robotics engineers tend to display distinct personalities: "They tend to be investigative individuals, which means they're intellectual, introspective, and inquisitive. They are curious, methodical, rational, analytical, and logical. Some of them are also realistic, meaning they're independent, stable, persistent, genuine, practical, and thrifty."[26]

## Working Conditions

Robotics engineers work in a variety of settings, depending on which industry they are in and the particular project they are working on. Some work in offices or research labs. Others work in factories, at universities, or from home offices. A robotics engineer who works in the health care industry might also make frequent visits to hospitals or clinics that use robotic devices and equipment.

## Employers and Earnings

The companies and businesses for whom robotics engineers work are quite diverse. Among the manufacturers that either already use robots or are in the process of installing them are food packaging companies and the makers of cosmetics, electronic parts, paints, adhesives, medications, construction materials, firearms, and cars and trucks. Among the many facilities that increasingly use robots and therefore require the services of robotics engineers are large farms, where robots pick fruits and vegetables and even pull up weeds; hospitals, where sophisticated robots aid surgeons in operating on patients; the military, where robots disarm bombs and carry supplies; and space programs, where robots are used in orbiting satellites, on space stations, and as landers and rovers that explore other planets and their moons.

In addition to these businesses, one fast-growing industry that employs robotics engineers is the delivery-drone business. According to Probot, a robotics company based in the Philippines,

> Delivery drones are flying robots that can transport items from one place to another. They're faster, cheaper, and more environmentally friendly than traditional methods of delivery. Some companies use them in their warehouses, while others have implemented drone deliveries directly to customers. In customer service applications like Amazon Prime Air . . . drones will drop off packages on your doorstep within 30 minutes after you order something online — that's way faster than anything you could get from UPS or FedEx![27]

## New Robotics Engineers: Should You Join a Start-Up Company or a Big Corporation?

"It really depends on your financial situation. If you have the bandwidth to join a startup, go for it. Do it now before you . . . have a laundry list of bills [to pay each] month. Corporate organizations are definitely going to provide you with security; they're going to provide you with a paycheck every day. . . . But if you're early in your career and have the bandwidth, choose a startup. . . . [With] the amount of funding going around right now, you're never going to see a better [chance to join a start-up]."

—Wesley Kennedy, surgical robotics expert

Quoted in Robotix with Sina, *Interview with Renowned Surgical Robotics Recruiter Wesley Kennedy*, YouTube. www.youtube.com/@RobotixwithSina.

Trained robotics engineers are needed to design these drones, build them, maintain and repair them, and work on designs and prototypes of next-generation robotic drones.

As for the salaries earned by robotics engineers, these also vary widely. Pay usually depends on factors such as level of education and experience, the size of the company, and the degree of complexity of the robots being designed and built. The average annual earnings for members of the profession in 2023–2024 was about $88,000. According to CareerExplorer, salaries for robotics engineers usually range from as low as $59,000 to as high as $165,000.

## Future Outlook

The field of robotics is expanding and will likely continue to do so in the years ahead. This is because numerous sectors of society are rapidly becoming more automated than ever before. And that means more and more robots will be needed, along with robotics engineers to create and maintain them.

There are various projected growth rates for the field of robotics engineering in the decade or so following 2024. One estimate, reported by the *Washington Post* in 2023, came from industry insiders who expect a 9 percent growth rate into the 2030s. This is well above the average growth rate for all professions.

## Find Out More

### Association for Advancing Automation (A3)

www.automate.org

A3 is North America's biggest private group that advocates for automation in society. It promotes the work of over thirteen hundred organizations involved in robotics and artificial intelligence. The A3 website provides news about advances in automation and lists upcoming conferences and webinars about robotics.

### IEEE Robotics & Automation Society (RAS)

www.ieee-ras.org

The RAS strongly supports research in the fields of robotics and automation and the sharing of scientific knowledge gained by that research among all members of the scientific community. Its website presents the latest news about the robotics field and offers detailed information about educational opportunities for would-be robotics scientists.

### International Federation of Robotics (IFR)

https://ifr.org

The IFR's goals are to strengthen and promote the robotics industry worldwide and to foster international cooperation among companies and governments that are striving to use robots to automate. The IFR website contains much detailed information about what robots do and the development of new robotic systems around the world.

# Environmental Scientist

## What Does an Environmental Scientist Do?

The multifaceted work of environmental scientists focuses on identifying, controlling, and when possible eradicating various pollutants and other threats to the global environment and, by extension, to public health. Typically, these researchers collect water, soil, and air samples; analyze those samples; compare the results to similar data gathered by other scientists; and draw general conclusions from the overall mass of data.

Environmental scientists regularly write reports in which they present their findings to the agencies they work for, government officials, the media, and the general public. In addition, members of the profession develop strategies designed to eliminate, or at least reduce, the impact of problems such as water and air pollution. Beyond that, some environmental scientists get involved in advising government officials about how to alter existing environmental and health policies with the goal of safeguarding public health.

Considering the enormous extent of numerous kinds of pollution plaguing modern society, scientists, a majority of government officials, and most members of the public agree that the work of environmental scientists is extremely important. In the words of Gayatri Kanungo, an environmental scientist at the World Bank, an international financial institution headquartered in Washington, DC:

> Nature and its ecosystems are central to healthy human existence. Keeping our planet healthy and resilient, therefore finds significant relevance, particularly as we are slowly emerging from the devastating impacts of the global COVID-19 pandemic. Globally complex interactions, including climate change impacts, are leading to increasing vulnerabilities in nature and jeopardizing livelihood prospects for millions of people across nations.[28]

One of the chief goals of environmental scientists, Kanungo says, is to reduce the negative impact of these threats. For her own part, she says that at present she is focusing on refurbishing and bringing back areas that over time have been stripped of greenery, farmland, and clean water by both climate change and rampant industrial development.

## A Typical Workday

Workdays for environmental scientists typically vary because they often have to accomplish a number of short-term duties in fairly rapid succession. These can include collecting water, soil, or air samples from a given area in the morning hours, followed by laboratory analysis of the samples; phone calls; library research; meetings with colleagues; travel by car, plane, or boat; or a combination of three or four such activities in the afternoon. In fact, environmental scientists frequently have so many duties to perform in a short time frame that a seven-to-eight hour workday is not sufficient to do the job properly. So putting in overtime is a common feature of the profession. Kanungo confirms this scenario by describing her own situation:

A typical day, which can stretch to 10–12 hours, is a mix of remote meetings with clients in developing countries; brainstorming with team members and external partners; and/or advisory for crisis management, project/policy reviews, and strategy development etc. My work also includes traveling across the globe for international meetings [and] project related work in countries including meeting [government officials], [scientific] partners, and [leaders of] communities—all towards supporting sustainable development goals.[29]

## Education and Training

Environmental scientists must have considerable expertise in scientific research and analysis and understand how to use advanced technological tools to gather and test samples. Entry-level positions for the profession require at least a bachelor's degree in environmental science, chemistry, microbiology, physics, oceanography, or soil science. Coursework typically includes chemistry, geology, biology, physics, hydrology, geology, waste management, geography, environmental policy, public administration, computer modeling, and data analysis. As in other science professions, advancement usually requires a master's degree or doctorate.

Regardless of which degree one seeks, many college programs in environmental science include an internship, also called a practicum. In it, the student aids a working scientist in an ongoing project. This provides valuable hands-on experience in the profession. American University in Washington, DC, for example, offers several annual internships, including one sponsored by the Smithsonian Environmental Research Center. In it, students help experts with land conservation projects on the shores of nearby Chesapeake Bay.

## Identifying the Effects of Harmful Substances

"My main area of research is to see whether or not there are any health effects from pesticide exposures at the general level that many people are exposed and whether there are any health effects or not during fetal development. . . . These pesticides that we are looking at are insecticides that have been widely used in homes in the United States. . . . Because of the results in laboratory animals, it seemed prudent to look in a human population to see whether there were any effects and hopefully we wouldn't find them."

—Robin M. Whyatt, Columbia University scientist

Quoted in Annenberg Learner, "Interview with Robin M. Whyatt," 2024. www.learner.org.

## Skills and Personality

Among the hard skills an environmental scientist should have or develop, probably the most important is a capacity for absorbing large amounts of scientific data and analyzing it. Several soft skills are essential as well. First is the ability to solve unexpected problems when they arise, because nature is filled with human-wrought pollution, and environmental scientists inevitably face challenges in eliminating such contamination. Self-discipline is also important because sometimes environmental scientists work alone. And at such times they must remain motivated to complete a project that takes a lot of time and effort. However, at other times environmental scientists work as members of team, so they must also possess interpersonal skills.

Especially crucial are communication skills, because environmental scientists are frequently called on to show and explain their findings to other scientists, government officials, and the public. This ability to communicate clearly includes both verbal and writing skills. Kanungo points out the importance of good writing skills in the profession: "[One needs] writing skills to match the needs of the work. While writing was something I always enjoyed, I put particular emphasis on learning the subtle nuances to help understand differences between, say, an academic research paper and a policy note. This is easily learnt with diligence and practice."[30]

## Working Conditions

Environmental scientists tend to work in four primary settings. One is offices, where they hammer out plans for cleaning up some sector of the environment, compile their findings, and write reports. Sometimes they work in the field, gathering samples. Environmental scientists also work in labs, where they analyze samples taken from the field. Finally, many environmental scientists spend at least some time giving lectures or briefing government officials.

## Employers and Earnings

Many environmental scientists work for federal, state, or local governments. In this capacity, they might advise elected officials or nonelected individuals who work for various government agencies on issues related to the environment. Those leaders might want to know about businesses that are not following the laws surrounding the safeguarding of the environment, for instance. Environmental scientists can provide this type of information. Other environmental scientists work for companies that provide consulting services to various businesses.

According to the Bureau of Labor Statistics (BLS), in 2022–2023 roughly 26 percent of environmental scientists worked for state governments, 14 percent worked for local government agencies, and 7 percent worked for the federal government. Another 21 percent worked for companies offering consulting services. The rest worked freelance, offering their services to companies or agencies that need them for only a single project.

Environmental scientists collect and analyze water, soil, and air samples, comparing their results to similar data gathered by other scientists. Their findings can be used to help reduce or eliminate threats to health and the environment.

According to the BLS, EnvironmentalScience.org, and other online sources of employment data, the average yearly earnings for environmental scientists in 2022–2023 was roughly $84,000. The lowest-paid 10 percent of workers in the profession—generally those employed by state governments—made approximately $73,000 annually. In contrast, those in the highest-paid 10 percent—mainly those employed by the federal government—earned about $109,000.

## Future Outlook

The BLS and similar employment data resources say that the future for environmental scientists appears to be stable and promising. In 2022–2023, the BLS estimates, there were about 80,500 members of the profession in the United States. And that figure is projected to grow steadily at least into the early 2030s. Until then,

## An Environmental Scientist Discovers a Passion for the Job

"[In my early days in this occupation] I began to seriously wonder about the interconnectedness of science and nature, particularly as my doctoral work on biologically producing pharmaceuticals also allowed me to look into the potential negative impacts of release of pharmaceutical waste into the environment. These experiences were subtly driving me towards opportunities . . . that could connect me with [the] environment and people in [my native] India . . . to explore and establish a career that could feed my passion [as an environmental scientist]."

— Gayatri Kanungo, World Bank environmental scientist

Quoted in Interview Portal, "Environmental Interview," July 5, 2022. https:// theinterviewportal.com.

there should be close to 7,000 job openings per year for environmental scientists, the BLS states.

One reason for this projected future growth in the ranks of environmental scientists is that public interest in the health of the earth's environment has been increasing in recent decades. This is attributable partly to repeated stories in the national news media about big corporations dumping hazardous waste in lakes and streams and humanity's ongoing pollution of the oceans. There is also the accelerating onrush of climate change. That factor alone is helping fuel the need for more environmental scientists who will aid in mitigating the negative effects of that expanding planetary dilemma. As a spokesperson for EnvironmentalScience.org puts it:

> When things like resource shortages, extreme weather events, and sea level rise brought on by climate change start disrupting supply chains and hitting corporations

where it hurts, all of a sudden you start seeing huge invest-ments in the search for solutions. This is what it's come to, and it's resulted in a surge in green jobs around the country, in almost every sector of both industry and gov-ernment.[31]

## Find Out More

### American Geosciences Institute (AGI)

www.americangeosciences.org

The AGI's main role is to provide researchers who study and seek to save the planet, including environmental scientists, with up-to-date information about ongoing work in their fields. The AGI website features information about how to get educated in the geosciences and news about the annual Earth Science Week.

### National Association of Environmental Professionals (NAEP)

www.naep.org

The NAEP acts as a resource for environmental scientists, help-ing guide them through obtaining an education, finding a job, and achieving excellence in their work. The NAEP website has a job board and provides information about annual conferences and workshops.

### National Institute of Environmental Health Sciences (NIEHS)

www.niehs.nih.gov

The NIEHS promotes and funds efforts by environmental scien-tists and others to sustain and hopefully improve the health of the earth's environment. The NIEHS website provides information about the institute's range of job opportunities and training and research programs.

# Source Notes

### Introduction: Skills Needed to Tackle Unanswered Questions

1. H.E. (Gene) Smith, "How I Became an Astronomer," Center for Astrophysics and Space Sciences, May 1, 2000. https://casswww.ucsd.edu.
2. Michelle Thaller, *Student of the Stars: How Do You Become an Astronomer?*, YouTube, 2020. www.youtube.com/watch?v=c1ZW3nVfe5A.
3. Bureau of Labor Statistics, "Fast Growing Science Occupations," March 8, 2024. https://blog.dol.gov.
4. Quoted in Kristin Burnham, "7 Professional Skills All Scientists Need," Northeastern University, May 20, 2020. https://graduate.northeastern.edu.

### Epidemiologist

5. Quoted in *U.S. News & World Report*, "Epidemiologist/Medical Scientist Overview," 2024. https://money.usnews.com.
6. Seema Yasmin, "Disease Detectives Investigate Outbreaks at Home and Abroad," *Scientific American*, 2014. https://blogs.scientificamerican.com.
7. Bureau of Labor Statistics, "How to Become an Epidemiologist," September 6, 2023. www.bls.gov.
8. Ingrid Monteiro, "What Does an Epidemiologist Do?," Indeed, October 4, 2022. www.indeed.com.

### Computer Hardware Engineer

9. Quoted in Interview Portal, "Apple Hardware Engineer Interview," October 29, 2018. https://theinterviewportal.com.
10. Quoted in Quora, "What Do You Do in a Day as a Computer Hardware Engineer?," 2024. www.quora.com.
11. James M. Tobin, "Hardware Engineer Career Overview," Computer Science.org, October 21, 2023. www.computerscience.org.
12. Aaron Kim, "Computer Hardware Engineers: Duties, Skills, and Salary," Indeed, September 24, 2023. www.indeed.com.

13. Kim, "Computer Hardware Engineers."
14. Bureau of Labor Statistics, "Computer Hardware Engineers: Similar Occupations," April 17, 2024. www.bls.gov.

## Microbiologist

15. Quoted in Science Buddies, "Science Careers: Interview with Mary Burtnick." www.sciencebuddies.org.
16. Quoted in Science Buddies, "Science Careers."
17. Bureau of Labor Statistics, "How to Become a Microbiologist," April 17, 2024. www.bls.gov.
18. Quoted in Science Buddies, "Science Careers."
19. Quoted in Science Buddies, "Science Careers."
20. Quoted in Justine Dees, "How to Spark Interest in Microbiology: Dr. Dave Westenberg," *Joyful Microbe*, April 22, 2021. https://joyfulmicrobe.com.

## Animal Scientist

21. Quoted in Ashley Patterson, "Where Passion Meets Science," Agrilife Today, May 8, 2024. https://agrilifetoday.tamu.edu.
22. Michigan State University, "Why Animal Science." www.canr.msu.edu.

## Robotics Engineer

23. CareerExplorer, "What Does a Robotics Engineer Do?," 2024. www.careerexplorer.com.
24. Robotics Career, "What Does a Robotics Engineer Do?," April 12, 2023. www.roboticscareer.org.
25. Quoted in Lillian Chen, "Meet Christine Fuller: Robotics Mechanical Engineer at NASA Jet Propulsion Laboratory," LinkedIn, January 4, 2018. www.linkedin.com.
26. CareerExplorer, "What Does a Robotics Engineer Do?"
27. Probot, "Top 10 Industries Utilizing Robots and Robotics," 2023. www.probotcorp.com.

## Environmental Scientist

28. Quoted in Interview Portal, "Environmental Interview," July 5, 2022. https://theinterviewportal.com.
29. Quoted in Interview Portal, "Environmental Interview."
30. Quoted in Interview Portal, "Environmental Interview."
31. EnvironmentalScience.org, "Environmental Science Careers," 2024. www.environmentalscience.org.

# Interview with a Scientist

Robyn Stanfield is a scientist at a biomedical research institute in San Diego, California. She has worked as a scientist for over thirty-five years. She answered questions about her career by email.

**Q: Can you describe the scientific work you do?**
**A:** I am a scientist who studies the structures of proteins using a technique called X-ray crystallography. The structures are then used to better understand how a protein works, and often are used to help design drugs that interact with the protein. To determine the structures, we have to first purify the protein we are interested in and then find conditions under which the protein will form crystals. We then aim a highly focused beam of X-rays at the crystal. The crystals act much like a prism, with the X-rays split into many separate X-ray beams due to interaction with the electrons in the protein crystal. These "diffracted" X-rays are captured on a detector, where we measure their position and intensity and then use a mathematical formula . . . to calculate an electron density map. These maps look very similar to a topographic map but show geographical features of the protein. We then build a model of the protein based on the electron density map. The finished protein structures are included in manuscripts describing what the protein looks like and how we think it works. The models are always deposited in the Protein Data Bank [a repository of information about the 3-D structures of proteins and other large biological molecules that are essential for research and education]. I usually study proteins, but DNA, RNA, small compounds, and peptides can also be studied with X-ray crystallography.

**Q: Why did you choose to work in this area of science?**
**A:** I studied chemistry as an undergraduate in college, and then went on to obtain a doctoral degree in chemistry. While in graduate school I became interested in the field of crystallography because I was fascinated with how a single protein structure could answer many different biological questions that were otherwise difficult to answer.

**Q: Can you describe your typical workday?**
**A:** On a typical day I spend part of my time working in the lab and part of my time working on a computer, writing manuscripts or working with data from a diffraction experiment. Several times a month we measure diffraction data from our crystals at a facility called a synchrotron that produces very intense X-ray beams. Unfortunately, some proteins are difficult to purify, some never crystallize, and some crystals don't diffract X-rays. In these cases, we try to change the protein itself, or the way we are purifying it, or the chemical mixture used to obtain crystals. I also spend time writing and reviewing manuscripts and writing grant proposals and progress reports to obtain funding for our experiments.

**Q: What do you like most about your job?**
**A:** The most exciting part of my job is when we obtain beautiful diffraction data for a new protein crystal and then get to see what the protein looks like.

**Q: What do you like least about your job?**
**A:** My least favorite thing to do at work is to wash beakers and flasks used in protein purification.

**Q: What personal qualities do you find most valuable for this type of work?**
**A:** To carry out any kind of scientific research you need to be very patient, creative, and persistent. I often go for months working very

hard in the lab but obtaining no positive results—either the protein can't be purified, or crystals won't grow, or crystals don't diffract, so I have to think of new ways to tackle these problems and then alter the experimental procedure to try to obtain better results.

**Q: What advice do you have for students who might be interested in this career?**

**A:** If you are interested in X-ray crystallography or any other sort of structural biology, you need to go to college and possibly to graduate school. There are many chemistry- and biology-related majors that can prepare you for this career.

# Other Jobs in Science

Astronaut
Astronomer
Biochemist
Biologist
Biophysicist
Cartographer
Chemist
Climate scientist
Computer programmer
Ecologist
Electrical engineer
Energy engineer
Food scientist
Forensic scientist
Geneticist

Hydrologist
Laboratory technician
Land surveyor
Marine engineer
Mechanical engineer
Meteorologist
Nanotechnologist
Nuclear engineer
Oceanographer
Paleontologist
Pharmacologist
Physicist
Seismologist
Soil scientist
Veterinarian

Editor's note: The online *Occupational Outlook Handbook* of the US Department of Labor's Bureau of Labor Statistics is an excellent source of information on jobs in hundreds of career fields, including many of those listed here. The *Occupational Outlook Handbook* may be accessed online at www.bls.gov/ooh.

# Index

# Picture Credits

# About the Author

Classical historian, amateur astronomer, and award-winning author Don Nardo has written numerous volumes about scientific topics, including the Smithsonian Institution's *Destined for Space* (winner of the Eugene M. Emme Award for best astronomical literature), *Tycho Brahe* (winner of the National Science Teaching Association's best book of the year), *Deadliest Dinosaurs*, *Black Holes*, *Tech Innovations Inspired by Nature*, and *The History of Science*. Nardo, who also composes and arranges orchestral music, lives with his wife, Christine, in Massachusetts.